Be Love

Love is all there is to this world which makes it what it is. Without it, the rest never makes sense. Using love as a tool for self realization.

Be Love

Dr Pallavi Kwatra

ISBN : 978-81-222-0600-5

Be Love

Subject: Poetry

1st Published in Orient Publishing 2017

Published by
Orient Publishing
(A division of Vision Books Pvt. Ltd.)
5A/8 Ansari Road, New Delhi-110 002
www.orientpaperbacks.com

Cover Design by Vision Studio

Printed at Yash Printographics, Noida

Printed on Cholrine-free eco-friendly paper

Dedicated to
the Guru, light & love.....

I am deeply grateful to my spiritual master, Renoo Ji for her inspirations and love, along with Dr Sampath Chandra Prasaad Rao for his beautiful preface and friends, Dr Tina M Benson and Ruhh Adhya for their kind and heartfelt words.

Preface

We know of love as ecstasy and longing, courage and grace, pain and joy and much much more. All that we learn in a lifetime is taught in the classroom of love. Who then is a better teacher than love to help us blend with our source? Love spurs us on an enchanting soul search journey where all ideas of good, bad, right or wrong dissolve in its effulgent light. The truth of god is unveiled and the heart merely becomes a spring of overflowing compassion. The beloved is an instrument to unleash our greatness and all our deep recesses that seemed scary and unknown are illuminated with its light. Why seek to know our source when love has blessed us with its presence and imparted us freedom from all about knowing. Just flow in surrender and all that ever needed to be discovered crystallizes clearly in the mirror of love. All miseries and pain dissolve in the warm embrace of the beloved and the soul is healed of its age old scars. The lover is only a messenger of our own soul self that comes to aid us in our journey of discovering the truth. In mystic ways, love coaches us to be a patron of beauty and become what an enlightened human being ought to be. I was also busy in my mundane material world, until one day suddenly, I was lifted off my feet by the mighty wings of love and that heralded my journey of self discoveries. Now, I soar higher and bask in its warmth to be "BLISS" infinite. Unlike love being merely a romantic adventure, love became a beacon to show me, "myself". It opened my experiences to other spatial dimensions where communion was a quality of the spirit and communication merely a vestigeal tool. This book is all about the ways and means love became my promising guide and god to emerge me from the abyss of misery.No religion or saint could take me where love guided my steps to, And I am only humbly, in gratitude for the greatest blessing of all lifetimes... in the orgasm of these manifold experiences, words were my only savior. Though deeply, I knew the futility of this expression to talk about the magnificence of it all, I was rendered as a mere instrument to this grand majestic tenderness. As I set forth to write this book, I was inspired by many influences. So, it would be ungrateful if I don't take this opportunity to express my heartfelt gaiety at these incitements. A divine plan almost often is a platform on which many characters appear at suitable times to play their designated roles. I was PLAIN lucky, that I was chosen. Spiritual workout in the form of reikI and other practices mellowed my heart and made me available and open to this overflowing grace. I am, and will eternally be indebted to my spiritual masters, Master, Renoo ji to be able to keep me constantly drowned and soaked in her infinite love, compassion and guiding light. amongst the many things love taught me, the most valuable lesson was to "let go". It seemed contradictory and it took me a whole lot of processing to do this 'letting go'. They say love is eternal. I don't really know coz love took me a full circle where it showed me passion, longing, essence at one end of the spectrum and pangs of loss and death like grief at the other. At the end of it however, it taught me the futility of possession, only to experience it full on, and then move on with gratefulness in one's heart. It showcased to me the greatest truth, that "nothing lasts forever" and one need not cling to anything or anyone. This has liberated me to a great extent and challenged my belief systems of love, integrity and the more so called heavy proclamations. Love, is not here to chain us, it is here to break all barriers, all identifications, theologies and allow us a freedom infinite where exchange is only "joy" without any tags. Another valuable realization was love's global encompassing ability. The grace of love's demeanor is that it will make you available to all ,from the point when you had started with only one. Compassion and universal identification are the final culmination of a divine communion. It cannot be restricted to merely two bodies, souls or individuals. It has to fuse itself into the eternal truth where all identifications are shed like a snake's old skin. I had set out on a spiritual rendezvous and I landed at the doorsteps of love. It's there that I learnt that the whole journey was all about love and returned the seeker to it again, again and yet, again. In many ways, the lessons were encrypted and retold until they got deeply imprinted and led to final liberation. Also, a great succor was to know that each of us are equally eligible to this universal humbling experience without any pre set qualifications or credentials. The great mystic SufI poet Jelaluddin RumI quotes, "Be certain in the religion of love, there are no believers or non believers...love embraces all alike..."

"In your light, I learn to love
In your beauty, how to make poems.
You dance inside my chest,
Where no one sees you,
But sometimes I do,
And that sight becomes this art."

The journey

There was once a time when I used to be a hard core skeptic and analytical in my approach to anything and everything. That was before I knew this author. I met Pallavi a couple of decades ago in medical school, but I really came to know her only a few years back when we chanced upon a re-acquaintance, that blossomed into a deep friendship. Over many long conversations, Pallavi led me to the fact that there was another way of looking at things that was contrary to logic but not necessarily illogical. She often spoke of emotions, passions and such sentiments. More importantly she spoke of "Love" like Love was all there is. I would have been the last person on earth who could write a preface to a book like this if not for the fact that my association with her left me utterly influenced with her ideas. Left with the onerous task of doing justice to a book on Love that has come out of the mind of a literary genius who is forever in Love, I decided to do nothing more than to pen my take on the subject and see if it holds good.

The way I look at it, Love is as old as life itself. Perhaps,Even older. All through the long history of existence, the overwhelming force that permeated everything is indeed Love. Fourteen billion years back, there was perhaps nothing except an all pervading intelligence, what we might call God. Like a mother would bring into existence her child enduring a painful birthing, so did the Creator deliver the Cosmos for no other reason but Love. Love, therefore, can be deemed as the most original and ultimate amongst all emotions and expressions.
Ten billion years passed by before the seed

of Life came into fruition, perhaps as a manifestation of the collective torment of the lifeless in the Creation to experience a miracle; to bring forth a meaning to its automated forms. With life somehow infused into the creation, nature now moved forward consciously. The creation created. And procreated. Simple life evolved into intelligent forms and yet this bubble of an intelligence was happening inside the Omnipresent. Love was at the core of both the levels. Inside the cosmos, Love touched lives and entwined them into union. And with union, life became a self-sustaining permanence. Since love gave birth to life, it had to also nurture it. And so it did. Love burst into myriad forms. While the love of a lover created life, that of a parent sustained it. That of a companion led to networking, colonization and consolidation of life. Every species on earth survived and proliferated on the bedrock of Love.

With the evolution of life, love evolved too. Man made his debut about 3 million years back. Despite his intelligence or may be owing to it, he could not handle the unfathomable power of this compelling emotion. It was but natural that this powerful entity could vividly captivate man's imagination to the point of obsession, even insanity. Man loved madly. He cried for it and even died for it. Expressions of Love brought out the best of his capabilities and virtues. He was at his creative best. However, when he could handle Love nor more, he developed in him its antithesis called Hate. Epic wars fought for Love or Hate. Man, all powerful and firmly seated in the center of all creative activity, earned himself the dubious distinction of becoming the only living entity who could kill and destroy in the name of Love and Hate. Thus Love had come a full circle. What was meant to bring forth life and nurture creation also extinguished it. But at the same time, another interesting phenomenon enveloped man. When the pinnacle of man's Love looked beyond the physical realm and sought the Divine Lover, the One who started it all, it took a whole new and yet unexplored form. That of devotion and surrender. This way Love came yet another full circle when the Love of the creation responded to the Love of the Creator. A sort of Self identification.

One experiences Love as much as one can understand and handle it. While Love is universal, it is also very individual, depending on the development of one's faculties. So every time the human intellect reflects over Love, it is a momentous occasion. With each introspection, we move closer to knowing ourselves. How much Love we are capable of and in what form? Is Love the only tool to unravel the mystery of the Creator? I don't know. But Pallavi thinks so. Her experiences of love are deep and her interpretations of them even more profound. Many of them have found expression in this book. Her spiritual nature makes her experience Love in a very fundamental way. She is an inherent lover, A seeker, A believer. It is impossible for her not to love. A heart as pure as hers makes it impossible not to love her back. So, when she writes a book on love there will expectedly be interpretations that have never been understood before, meanings never been discovered before. In this book Pallavi has painted love in intense shades. Her own angst has found manifestation through her pen flowering into a stirring expression of emotions and imaginations. This book apart from being an exhibition of her literary genius, is also an expression of who she actually is. An embodiment of love.

Dr. Sampath Chandra Prasad Rao

MS, DNB, FEB-ORLHNS, FEAONO

Fellowship trained in Skull Base Surgery.

Department of Otology & Skull Base Surgery,

Gruppo Otologico, Piacenza-Rome, Italy

sampath.prasad@gruppootoogico.it

www.gruppootologico.com

CONTENTS

The Densities.

The Densities

The Journey....

In surreal undertones,
and spills of careless shades,
I set out to paint and sculpt,
My hands a little frenzied,
My soul a little drunk,
I surrendered my authorities,
And rights of all ownership.
I thought...I'd see what truly
does "involuntary" mean?
I went a little furthur,
and then stood statue still,
I was asked to empty my pockets,
and undress all my scars.
and give it all away.

In total compliance,
I kneeled, bared of all pretensions,
feeling gay and free.
I had nothing to lose,
not even my fears.
Now, I knew true freedom,
and how creativity is born today.
A masterpiece now stands before me,
and credits raining on me.
But I know, the real prize
was to journey through it all....

The Inseparable Whole....

Within me, I am thousands,
That ache discovery.
Beyond the limits of the eye,
I exist; in multiple ways.

The intertwining roles,
The face that expresses oceans,
One would wonder at this enigma,
Of how could so many be in "singularity".

Conflicting corners of a single masterpiece,
The hue of colours blending in one.
Notes of music that thread into a song.
Overlapping borders of love and hate.
Sins and virtues; adorning the self.

The similies of chip and dale,
The opposites of mr jekyll and hyde.
Is rejection really a choice?
When all is an inseparable part of the whole...

I AM the.......

I am the flavor of your burning skies,
the taste of your ravishing passion,
I am the evenings you linger on,
and the prayers you awaken to.
I am the breath that exchanges life,
and the splashing blood in your fragile veins.
I am the bones that support your skin,
and the tear that salts your kind mouth.
ERADICATION of " me" is not a choice
I allow you to make.....

My return to you...

At the edge of an overhanging night,
When the stars have lulled the babies to bed,
And the birds are just about rising up,
When dawn has started twinkling at the horizon,
And the moon is disappointed, yet again,
Of not being able to meet it's sun.
When the silence and its echo,
Both have been merged as one,
Me, a lonely travellar
Sets forth on a sacred pilgrimage.
I know not, what better , my love ought do,
My journey of a million lifetimes
Safely returns "me"
to you...

The love I know of....

The love I know of has no colour or shape,
It spills on me and leaves me blessed.
It only senses, pulses and breathes,
Never judges or condemns.
When I am by myself,
It comes to assure me of eternal companionship.
When I am with others,
It reminds me of singularity and oneness.
Who or what guides my steps, I know not,
But he ensures that I manage my destination
well.

In grief and loss,
He embraces my sulks.
In joy and success,
He sips from my wine.
In agonies and fears,
He lulls me to sleep.
In waking moments,
He keeps me aware and grateful.
I only know of love...
The way he teaches me through his endless ways.

That one is you...

Silence is the altar in which I worship thee,
and tears the offerings of my ageing soul.
I know not what the trends of worship are,
nor the etiquettes of devotion.
I only know I hold back nothing,
and seek not any lusty cravings.
What you bless,
I pride at that
and what you don't,
I humbly suffer.
Who or what can ail my woes
or hang my fears unto death?
I know only 'one'
and that ONE is 'you'.

The mermaid......

When you board a mighty ship,
I"ll know this by the singing waves.
The constellations will lead you to me,
And the lighthouses guide your way.
The moon will shine on your shady deck,
And the sun make the icebergs melt.
In the depths of the ocean,
When you will reach...
I'll hypnotise
and allure
With melodies you have known before.
In enchanting beauty
I'll rise to the water's edge,
And woo you to unknown lands
Where time has lost its own presence,
And 'misplaced' is what the place is called.
The others might wonder,you are dead,
Only you will know your "anointed birth".

The taboos of proximity...

On an unexpected day,
When the setting for love was perfect,
You and I met.
The heart was in delight,
And the bodies in ecstasy, for discovery.
A long wait had preluded
This impending communion.
The words had brought us this far.
But now, they served no more.
A new journey awaited us
Where knowing would take new forms.
The boundaries had now to fade,
And the fences pulled down.
The beauty of love
Now seeks newer dimensions.
The wrinkle on your forehead
Was a un invited guest.

Where was the place of worry?
When love flourished all around?
In deep contemplation, you spoke
In words that choked on tears.
You had been struck, un alarmed
By the taboos of proximity.
Love has a strange silent strength
Even when it seems fragile like a flower.
And with the patience of a saint
I declared that I'd wait
Until the pangs would vanish and wither
To the rains of my love.....

Thus, is how I love you...

The sun sets into
the distant valleys
in a longing to
swounder its grandeur
To be taken over in a way like this,
Thus, Is how I love you.
The dew drops dance on the rose petals,
As if they were eternal and free.
The sun comes along and seizes their life,
Thus, is how I love you.
The meandering river is gay at heart,
And flows without maps into its sea,
The way it never loses its way,
Thus, is how I love you.
The caterpillar metamorphoses painfully,
To live it's newly found form.
Its life is short, but sweet,

Thus, is how I love you.
The past gives way to the present,
the young to the old.
Spring remembers to follow winter,
Thus, is how I love you.
Certain secrets are for a lifetime,
They stay concealed,
In the space between the shadow and the soul.
Thus, is how I love you.
Quench is here to guide the thirst,
Lighthouses to the lost ships,
Forgotten memoirs to scald the heart,
Thus, is how I love you.
Reasons are useless,
Words are futile,
My miseries know of only you as god,
Thus, is how I love you

I know not...

To write on subjects, more.
I Searched my heart,
Sought my soul,
Voices echoed in choruses of light,
I know not, to write on new or more.
When all I hear is love, so bright.
Rest of it are mere shadows.
Love is the climate of my soul.
And songs of it flood my lips.
How can poetry be otherwise?
All that brims is the one that spills!
Kindle in me some other storm
That has a fervor greater than love.
I am merely a canvas nude,
What you adorn me is what I pride.
Until then, let me speak of love
Because to know, and yet fake,
Would only amount to sin............

The erotic paraphernalia

On the banks of a glittering lake,
At the impending dusk,
We arrive intoxicated to love,
The souls stuporous,
The bodies in new shade,
We entangle to love,
Pressing ourselves closer.
How can the bodies touch more
Than what the soul mingles on?
This new discovered lust,
Is in real an ancient desire
Which leads us to this bonding intimacy,
The body a little shy,
The awakened mind,
Choose to find succor
In an entwined embrace,

Ah! These peaks of lust
Thrusting against the banks of shuddering
Bodies,
We are driven by a desire for oneness.
Let's ride on this long
Until we discover "union".

The Alchemy

Submerged under the debris of morality,
Breathe some forbidden zones
Where every desire is a chaste homage,
Every attachment, a trespass to freedom,
Where love is not in confinement,
And the bodies embalm in a muted embrace.
The solace of whining souls
Rests in their terminal fusion,
Are we in recognition of
These messages from beyond?
Are we in symbolic unison
Of mind, body & spirit?
Where every longing, every proximity,
Every anguish, every affinity
Is a part of the divine alchemy.

The love Saga

In the epitomes of a buried past,
Lie the dormant seeds of fate.
They sprout once In a while,
And bloom like lotuses in our muddy ponds.
We welcome them with surrender,
Harvest them with faith.
The relics of love stand untarnished
From eons of a timeless time.
When every memory is a divine lineage,
And every desire, a chaste acclaim,
Through this time travel across universes,
The story has been again refreshed.
The hidden palladium of our love story
Now beckones us with open arms.
Are we ready to believe in this miraculous gift
That has been bestowed as divine grace?
Are we ready to enact our roles
In this brand new love saga?

The Cupcakes

For the impassioned heart, distance only acts as a bridge. It is as if they never parted
The ecstacy is mummified for all eternity.

I send my roots deep into the soil of your soul
In turn you nourish me with the awakenings of love.

I shall pretend to die
So that you breathe into me,
the dreams of my life.

The early morning dewdrops danced on the petals of the newly bloomed rose
It had waited all night to show off its beauty.

If you were by my side
I'd fly to the moon on a single wing.

The windchimes of my heart broke into a cry
They had heard you arriving, much before you
came.

Even the rainbows lose their sheen when we glow
in our love
What use are of candles
when the sun has arrived on the horizon?

All miseries are effaced at the touch of your lips
Now, I'm only light.

There's something very sensuous about the way
you engulf my fingers in your clasp.
All of me surrenders to lust.

How meticulously you maintain the annals of our love
I'm only obsessed with creating it.

Being lustful for your beloved is a sin they say
To me, It is only a pious ritual in the worship of love.

Nothing or no one ever gets lost
All love is recycled in the universe.

Water can never be clasped. The only way to hold it is to gently cup it in your palms
Love demands a certain delicacy in being possessed.

I have structured invisible cords of light from your heart to mine.
Now, no spaces remain un illuminated.

Why wait for the bodies to know
Hasn't the soul tasted love's ecstasy, yet?

The ripples on the surface are often silent
messengers of the undercurrents below
What lies beneath is thirsting discovery and
praise.

My aura boasts of badges of love
I had been touched by the light.

Don't be kind to me. Give me your compassion.
Kindness only fuels the ego
Compassion mellows us both.

When I see you in pain, each sore of mine also
begins to suppurate
God, how grateful, I am, to be so close.

I see your life being wasted in the futility of
service.
Then I see the sun. And I know that the giver does
not judge the receiver.

You always give to others a part of you, no
matter whether they care
What you give to me, I have enshrined
forever.

Impregnate my every cell with your love
They have suffered sterility for eons.

When your lips come to kiss me, they
part almost as a reflex
It's a natural welcoming to the grace.

Lock your body with mine.
It's a sin to be away when I know that you have arrived.

Surrender all that's religious in you and make space to welcome love.
A scabbard can hold only a single sword.

Religions talk of virtues and sins
causing un necessary confusions
Rise above the chaos, to be only grounded in love.

Let me be the dancing tide in your ocean's lap
to emerge in mystic and carefree fashions and
then drown in your bosom to be free.

Touch me in any cell and all pulsations will
throb only of you
The sea has the same salt everywhere and the
flower, the same fragrance in all its petals.

I had been worthless all my life.
Suddenly, the world has awakened
to my presence
I have been here since time without beginning.
It was you
who showcased my genius to the world.

In the grave, your presence still throbs inside me
as if my heart has disobeyed to die.

As soon as you touch,
all my sensations come alive
In mystic dances
Your presence is an invitation to phenomenal
discoveries of the self.

I had been arrogant about my knowledge of the self
The lessons that your touch imparted have made me kneel in humility.

Take me on a pilgrimage to all your spaces.
I shall light in each of them, candles of my devotion.

Your hands have an unparallel intelligence
which ferries them to my seeking corners
It's your emanating springs gush to quench my pious thirst.

Much of me was untilled land
You harvested it to fertile flower and fruit.

You and I had risen together, at dawn
The dawn of our awakening...

If it were not for you
I'd remain unfound to love.

Until now, I had received divine grace in tiny fragmented bursts.
After you came, the real grandeur unleashed itself in full glory.
All words fail in the description of such bliss.

Your pristine love has complimented all the jumbled pieces of my being.
Now, I exist
Whole and complete.

Wonder what's the best time to make love??
At night, the stars keep peeking
and at dawn, the birds screech to interfere.

The flower had opened its petals delicately to
the butterfly
Who had waited in patience for the impending
communion.

Why seek enlightenment?
Love is better.

I stayed back
to sip a little leftovers from your cup
Your lips had given up on them, a while ago.

The shades of grey had been endangered
Love had proclaimed its arrival.

The stars truly revere the sun.
They surrender to it, everyday.

You come and practice the gymnastics of love
in the courtyard of my shabby abode
Magically, it transforms into the palace of my
dreams.

Why should I fall in love
When there are many opportunities to rise in it?

My fantasies of heaven come quite close to the
dim lit room where we had discovered love
In the deepest quarries are where the diamonds
are mined.

If I were my usual self, I'd try to dissuade you
out of love
However, each of us are more intoxicated than
the other.

I consented
to your hands to search all my attics.
The treasures that were discovered dazzled us
both.

I come to you as if I come to a shrine.
"Surrender" is my only offering.

Look no further after discovering love
All that needed discovery has known the light.

In my pledge of love
All vain promises to the self had dissolved.

Your aura screams of its ecstasy.
This has deafened me to the rest of the world.

I had set sail on unknown waters.
On losing my way, I ended up at your shore.
Now, many ships have come and gone.
But I reign, as a king on the island of your heart.

You sing me lullabies of love.
They echo into my farthest dreams.

You have splashed on my soul, the rainbows of your love.
The emboss on me is a grand insignia unto eternity.

I would rather not go
to visit the lovely landscapes of enlightenment
without you
Come and lead me to the beauty.

You are like the pied piper
Who woos all my miseries to demise.

Please engrave my promise of love on my grave.
Let me be reminded of it even on the days you
forget to light candles or offer flowers.

I tie my dreams to your wings
And see them soar every time you
ascend to the skies.

You undress the rags of old sorrows
Now there emerges from within, a novel light body
that blinds my soul with its scintillating aura.

When I started moving towards the light,
my legs were heavy and tired
And then you came...
Awaring me to the wings I had grown and
instilling in me, the courage to fly.

I come like a thirsty one
to drink from the spring
There, I see your reflection and am quenched
unto eternity.

When the petals of your lips part,
I gain entry into the kingdom of heaven
And become amnesic about my way back.

With great pride, I compose melodies and rush
to boast about them to you
Only to find you humming them to the buds in
your garden.

I sweat and toil on sunny roads
You come like the shades to succor my soul.

When life do us part, be sure to lend me a part
of your soul
I'll thrive on it, until we meet again.

I shall use the mortar of our communion as
foundation to create monasteries
Where I will educate disciples in the great
art of love.

All my leaves have been covered with dusts of suffering
Rain on me, your love to cleanse and sparkle me again.

You and I are like trees that grow side by side
On the outside, we stand tall and upright.
Below, our roots are entwined in deep love and interdependence.

Let the swirling winds of time and fate never uproot our juvenile sapling of love.
A majestic tree will then shade many in the years to come.

Make tiny labeled packets of your pains and place them on the shelves of my heart's safe
I shall lock them there and lose the key.

The wheel of time spins on,
endlessly
It inculcates in me,
the eternity of love.

Your love flows through the channels in my
orchards.
That's how I remain green and fragrant.

I strategize shortcuts to your heart, only
To discover me frolicking and playing there,
already.

I had been tilling my barren soils with tears
and sweat from eons.
Now, the crops of your love have finally grown,
rebelling against all fate filling my vision into
the distant horizons.

My love started as a tiny brook
with meager waters,
soon transforming
into a mighty river of majesty and splendor.
Now, it seeks only to merge into your ocean of bliss.

I was struggling to polish my crystals
until I mined in you
A sparkling diamond quarry.

I remember being arrogant
and never bowing in
prayer
Now, my life is a
living bible of love.

The gems of my words become stunning jewellry
Only when threaded in the golden strings of
your love.

Following the humming of my heart
that was intoxicated in the lust of love,
I reached your step.
The door was open.
I stepped in, to discover you kneeling, in prayer.
My search had culminated beautifully.

The stark separation between my ignorant
mundane life
and my life of miracles and grace
is marked by your appearance on my timeline.

You enamor me to the palace of your dreams
and enchant me with the luxuries of lust.

I am a simpleton
and you
The king of love.

Whenever I experience the pangs of silence
You come along
singing melodies of love.

I had read many books and listened to many
a teacher speak.
But nothing transformed my inner milieu.
It was your love that flooded me with the light
of the self.

Nothing except love makes sense to an ailing
heart.
The rest is all mundane.

You had left me and gone for a jiffy.
It gave me time to breathe your memories.

My life was over, my love was not.
I had an incentive to be born again.

They say that the ails of the heart never heal.
But I knew none after you held me in gaze.

When you cried, something extraordinary happened.
The skies of my heart witnessed shower and rains.

Where is the thread that links your heart to mine?
I shall replace it with anchors of steel.

My ears have deafened to the sounds of the world.
Now I listen only to the hummings of my heart.

Your pristine face had ripped me of all ideas of beauty.
I surrender all that I know before what you are.

You splash the colors of your soul on the canvas of my heart.
And all are in awe of the paintings we make.

Let me be the valley where you set your sun at
the end of a long painful day,
And emerge afresh the following morning to
light up the world.

I envy the bangles that adorn your wrists
They kiss your skin all the time
and fill your silent moments with tinkling
melodies.

Kindle in me the spark of love
Then I shall be empowered to light up the skies.

After my demise, all of me had withered except
my lips
They remained moist to receive your adieu.

How can you be anyone else's other than mine?
Have the stars ever belonged to the day?
They only know the bosom of the night from
which is born their twinkling splendor?

When death
deprives me the privilege of holding you in
embrace,
I shall send you the scented breezes of spring...

Today we were on a stroll in the garden, the
birds screeched their lungs out
Jealousy had turned them into riots.

Love had made me lighter than the clouds.
I was now closer to the kingdom of god.

All precepts of celibacy melt at the touch of
your lips.
Are not promises made only to be broken?

Sometimes
I am bewildered
by the way I instantly answer the questions
which had barely arisen in your heart
and your mind translated into words.
Our communications is not at the mercy of the
limping words.

I was an atheist until one fine day
When you lifted all the veils of ignorance from
god's presence.

With you beside me
never light up the candles.
They are undignified in the presence of the moon.

You come to pick me from the abyss of misery.
For me, there is no other 'god'.

Meeting you in this lifetime
is the greatest serendipity I know.
I never had been a believer in destiny till date.

If I could die making love to you,
Enlightenment would never delude me.

The god that I know of,
mimics you in beauty and grace
But it mimics
And "you are".

You bring to me the synchronicities of joys.
My soul has never known such happiness before.

You educate me every single day with the
chapters of love.
And I practice and perfect them in your eager
and unconditional acceptance.

I knew of love and I knew of god.
Now, I know of them as 'one'.

The light had disillusioned me all this time
And then you came,
bringing me the sun.

Now, the mundane prophesies of religion don't
ignite any passion in me.
My only religion is love.

Alas... this life of mine will also perish one day.
What can I offer you
more eternal than my love?

Why do you come to mourn at my grave?
Always remember,
all that goes around, comes around!

Everything I did, before I met you was profane.
It is only now that I am truly spiritual.

The warp & weft of my weave are nothing
But the crisscrossed multi-colored threads of
your love.

I was a sand grain, lost to the sea.
You found me and made me into a pearl.

All of me was bound in the miseries of life
Till you came and silently undid the knots.

Just when I was gasping at my last breath,
Your lips bestowed me with the gift of life.

Now, I freely converse with the flowers in the garden.
They speak the language that your love has educated me with.

On the few days that we don't meet,
I barely notice myself.

What vanity could be a match for your innocent smile?
The ornaments only serve the unequipped.

Where did you first step on returning home???
I'll make my temple there.

Now, I miss my loneliness
After you came, it never returns.

Many before me had drowned in the sea of love.
And yet,when you beckon
I 'm tugged to your shores.

The tides of my love flow incessantly towards
the shore of your being.
How long will you resist the tug?

I checked the oysters & shells at sea. All
the pearls in them were gone. I returned
disappointed to the shore
Only to be received by you studded with them.

Wonder when the days blend into starry nights
and the dawns emerge from the still moon?
I have been awake, only loving you...

When you are beside me
There can be no other 'sun'.

A little while ago, you had been mine,
and now your life beckons you
All I pursue is your journey back home...

After you have left
Your presence breathes.

I knew you looked beautiful today
My soul had sighed in your presence.

In the early hours, you snuggled out of bed for
a bath
I had waited to follow you, all night.

If you ask me how many times you crossed my
mind, i'd say once.
Coz you never really left.

I live in every moment that I spend in love.
I barely exist in the rest.

Just let me touch you now
Once, where you most reside...
Your heart.

I sit and cry at night, agonizing in your pain and grief.
And you ask me, at dawn, how restful was my sleep.

Your tears fall on my soul.
And I keep getting wealthier with the pearls.

You are my true patron.
Only you invest your love in me.

I was hesitant to walk on the sands of your heart
with my muddy feet.
That set you upon the task of bathing them clean.

My poetry is nothing
But the whispers of your love,
in my moments of silence.

How can I fail to notice anything that your eyes have touched?
The ordinary now sparkles like gold.

I compose
poetry and you live it the same.
It's like the great alchemy of the day and night.

If you had not attuned me into love
I'd merely be existing.

To depart is forbidden
All who enter my kingdom of love.

Your eyes are the most beautiful part of you.
They are the windows of the beauty in your soul.

The night has just dawned with beautiful eruptions of the stars, and the moon is lazily awakening to its unbothered beauty, and you lullaby me to sleep.
What a shame it would be, to not weave my dreams with these natural inspirations?

I had all the possessions one could dream of.
I sold them all to buy the bewilderment of love.

It took me lifetimes to awaken to love.
Now, there's no question of sleeping for a while.

Succumb to love, my dear.
Life might not offer you better.

Our love is the sacred space I enter,
everyday
Only to deepen my devotion to life.

You were my true north.
Whenever lost, I was guided by your light.

My path had been walked upon,
by many a traveler
But the footprints belonged, only to you.

I threw messages in bottles, to the sea.
And prayed to god, that they kiss your shores.

My words speak of my love
And my silences of it' s scars.

I got lost to the world
The day, I was found to love.

In the book of my life,
You are the full stop in the final paragraph.

I hope you have noticed
your footsteps on my sands, and the way I
guard them with my life
Against the kiss of the raging waves.

Which is my real world?
The one that I live in or the one that lives in
me?

The more I love you, the farther the others retreat.
What good am I to them, now?

Come and pull out the dagger from my heart.
Someone just left it, mid-way.

Love touches our core and brings to light, all that we are worthy of.
There is nothing more illuminating.

I am the tree that boasts of beautiful flowers & luscious fruits.
My riches are the gifts from the river on which, I grow.

The birds fly with conviction,
on the path, that is unseen to others.
Thus, I follow the road that leads to you.

Does a river plot to reach the sea???
It just goes about,
dancing merrily carving its path to bliss.

I am only adamant that you be my companion
on my trip to heaven.
Who's bothered about reaching, anyways?

This world has its own beauty and craziness
Will admire it
when I'm over with mine.

I engage in worldly affairs,
only to distract
myself from 'us'
Lest all days are spent only in the reverie of
our bliss.

I urge you to come with me to the dungeons of my fears
So that your light illuminates the deepest recesses of my darkness.

When I met you, I was awakened
From my slumbers of 'seeking'.

Now days, I find you in all my reflections
My mirror has got used to the two of us...

Sing and dance all you can and when you get weary, seek my warm refuge.
I shall prepare you for your next performance.

I tried cupping sand in my hands, and all of it was futile endeavor.
such was my effort in writing of our love.

Congratulations, my heart
You have birthed to love.

Illustrations of my heart are like landscapes of divinity.
The other paintings don't allure me anymore.

My heart has thrown up a coup
The pain had reigned there long.

Give me love sickness
I'll use it to heal the rest.

Surrender to love, my fragile heart
No one dares disobey the emperor.

Crooked are the routes that pain takes to empty out of my heart
Love is it' s guide on this perilous journey.

Behind closed doors,
I learnt life's greatest lessons
My teacher
was proficient in the knowledge of love.

Your presence inspires poetry in me
At one time, I was illiterate to the alphabets of love.

I wait
for us to orgasm together
What's the fun of travelling alone to the stars?

The ways your hands stroke me
are like the paintbrush of god
Masterpieces are sketched in every nook & corner.

The humming bird flutters with ecstasy around
the blooming flower, but sucks its nectar
delicately, causing no harm
Thus you come to make love to me.

At our horizon, we shall meet
Never to part.

Snowflakes fall on my window sill
and its chill has frozen my soul.
Come and be the sunshine
and warm me back to life.

I lust my eyes before they fall on you
It' s my silent tribute to your resplendent
beauty.

Keep your windows closed at night
Else, i'll avenge the moon who dares shine on
you.

Sickle my woes and leave behind only that is yours.
It's cleansing to de weed once in a while.

Thaw my heart; slowly to love.
A little more heat might melt it away.

Your love has frenzied me to some different space.
I strive to return to worldly life
and feel ecstatic, having lost the game.

I have been travelling all the way up, the darkness of the well.
Your light welcomes me to a brand new world.

Longings are for those who are cowards in love.
We only believe in conquering hearts.

Today, I dreamt of you as having aged.
My love for you graduated to another level.

Give me no clues that lead me out of you.
I am happy to spend eons, being lost.

Sometimes you cry
And my mouth knows the salt.

On your journey of self discovery,
pause at my stop for a breather.
Go no further
Coz you have finally arrived.

Look at the rainbows in your aura.
They are mere reflections of the light within.

When the light dims, you come and be my guest
Neighbors are always in envy of the radiance
that glows my humble abode.

Today the moon is crescent. In a few days, it shall be full.
That's how love ripens to time.

I'll infect you
Till the time you get sick with me.

Let not this night be in vain.
Today the moon is absent
It's time we light up the skies.

The breeze that's coming from your house has revealed your deepest secrets,
The stars have made portraits of you lazing half clad in bed,
The moon has been vying and hearing you sing.
Even though you are away, they all bring you to me.

In my temple
My altar is empty. Come and be my "god"
I'll sing hymns for you, everyday.

An angel and a butterfly befriended. The angel had a deficient wing and the butterfly had torn its better half.
Together, they soared on the skies of love.

The ripples on your lake are nothing
But my whispers of love to you.

Single out all your immoralities and dry them out in my sun.
Hang them back as virtues, once done.

The light had eluded me all this time, coz I was unprimed.
At your arrival, the preparations concluded in illumination.

On our nights of lovemaking, you ensure the
lamps lack oil in them
But, my dear, aren't you aware that I carry
with me, the suns?

Never underestimate the power of love,
Miracles are born of it, when tended with care.

I take your permission to sleep at nights
But my dreams beg not your consent.

Whatever you speak or do, all I believe is what
I see in your eyes.
When the sun is so glaring, why burn the oils?

Kindle in me
The candles of hope.
I will light them when those of faith and love
are burnt out...

My flame whispered to yours
"will you be mine?"
And your flame flickered and waned out
Surrendering itself to love.

In the halo of your flame, I reside unharmed.
It singes my sorrows without causing me burns.

You melt to my love as the wax melts to the flames.
Only in extinguishing ourselves, can we truly illuminate the other.

The refuge of love lulls me to sleep
Even when the blizzards of suffering rage at my door.

Today is special, indeed
You have come to drink from my waters.
All along, I had thirsted for this.

Don't waste your tears on me,
Keep the pearls for the aches of the world.

You grace me with your love
And crown me as emperor.
I was only a monk who had knocked, for alms.

Your waterfalls cascade and splash at my rocks.
Alas, one fine day
I'll have to yield.

Why do you pray, when all that you are
Is the biggest prayer?
Just witness your beauty in the mirror, at daybreak.

The hardwired patterns of my soul melt
In the furnace of your unconditional love.

I tried writing about love
Silence was my favorite pen...

Love is a strange thing!
It singes your soul, even when absent.

My soul is bare and stripped before you;
my body merely a puppet in your hands
All that I had believed as mine
has rebelled against me to join you.

We meet and part, then part and meet
I and love are like day and night.

When I think of me having caused you tears,
I know not what punishment suits me best.
Some sins would can never be paid for, no
matter how great the repentance.

Once, I had loved,
Now, I only pray to thee.

Every time your eyes close to shed a tear, the
sun is obscured by some fleeting clouds.
I pray for these shadows to be meager and
short.

I run along my borders to check for spills.
You had splashed me carelessly with your love.

I sit around you and bask in your warmth,
The rest only see my dazzling glow.

Death had taken me away from life
Now, I stand resurrected to love.

What I have discovered about love still remains
as a hidden mystery to many.
They had not waited patiently enough.

Your seeds in me have finally flourished
It took eons of nourishment to prepare this
stone.

Even when I close my eyes, your face is crystal
clear.
My tears had polished my mirror well.

Count your possessions before you fall in love
You might forget all about owning, later on.

You say that our love is deepening, but I find
no change
Ageless as it is, our love has always been this
agile.

I slip in quietly into the niche of your heart
And you are in awe of how full you are with me.

Each of my chandeliers were rusted and grim lit,
You came and polished them into jewels of
light.

We have walked this road earlier
and as we walk it again.
We marvel at our familiarity of its curves and
bends.

I am the lute who thirsts for your lips,
This longing is what sweetens my music.

Who looks at the world when you are by my side
Why strain at the gnats and swallow the camels?

My love for you is no longer an emotion.
It is an intensity that has eradicated the "me".

When you speak to me, I hardly hear your words,
My dazed mind is busy following the grace of your lips.

Against the background of the noises of the world, the silence of our love stands out as a stark separation.
White chalk marks are often visible only against dark blackboards.

My astute head only knows the conspiracies of love.
The other strategies, it surrendered to the world.

When you come dancing to me, my ecstasies stand paralyzed
They need to bow in reverence before the king.

The master appears
when the disciple is ready
And so does the beloved when the lover is!

You have sabotaged my heart and held me in siege.
Treat me with dignity before I succumb to your rule.

Since we met, my life has felt metamorphosis.
No one can enter love and remain unchanged.

Too many gateways are on my path
But I follow the one that leads to love.

After your arrival, my autobiography is extinct.
The "my" got lost forever to love.

Even the sun parts with its rays and the cloud
with its pearls.
May I be inspired by their magnanimity when
you leave me at the end of a night of love.

Your threads are woven into my fabric.
How will you seek your entity when it has
blended into mine?

I was an unremembered season
Until you made me a perennial climate.

I was like an ocean with raging waves and storms.
Now I am a silent lake,
where the ripples are infrequent occurences.

Now I can dream with open eyes.
That's your gift of new vision to me.

Very subtly you have come and displaced the old and worn out, "me".
Other than love, no clutter remains.

I weaved since lifetimes, and you came and un did all that.
Now, I stand naked, but grateful.

I feel no urge to share or conceal.
I am an open book before the reader of love.

I yearn to paint with your colors, the painting of my dreams.
The world has been longing for a masterpiece, since long.

The heart cringes
in pain and agony
at the demise of the beloved
Now who will rehabilitate
the orphan in me to love?

Seduce me only to love
The rest merely distracts for a while.

Love instantly lifts us to the heavens
Until now, we were heavy and chained.

There is no bigger pain than the agony of love
And yet, it is the one we longingly pine for.

Love comes to us as the swirling typhoon.
All that has existed
is blown away by its ferocity and fullness.

My beloved has left the dagger embedded in my soul,
It is a sweet reminder of the fact that I had once loved.

When our heart is full, our lives brim with miracles
Who knew that they ever existed before this?

Simple are the treasures I own
Love is priceless amongst them all.

I had sworn never to love,
You came and I forgot all about promises.

Now what is there that I can claim to be mine?
I auctioned it all to love.

Little blessings are due to life
big ones, due to love.

Consummate me unto love!
Its long since my virginity ached for it.

There are virtues I would die for and be called a martyr.
I'd rather choose love and be a simpleton.

You are like the cloud that hovers over the skies,
you shield me from the burns of the sun.

I know little about the world but I am a scholar of love.
I took my lessons from the teacher of surrender.

Facets of my being were demolished by love.
Amidst these ruins, I construct my sacred self.

Who says love is a soft wind that caresses your anguished soul?
It's the turbulent storm that sweeps away all that resists.

I keep sifting through your thoughts as if turning the pages of a book.
All your secrets lie naked before my peeking gaze.

Your respect and reputation are all at stake,
You have been trespassing too often through my brothel.

Sediments often settle after a little while of indifference.
Stop stirring and reconcile to love.

Most of my thoughts, I keep secret from the world,
Waiting for their ears to be attuned to the truth.

Unsung melodies are sweeter than the ones that adorn the lips
Let the beauty be fortified by the treasures of my heart.

I succumb to every wave in your ocean
And rise afresh and revitalized when I am done.

In every moon, there are shades of grey
So is my love when you are away.

I know of love and I know of loss
Love helps me to lose with dignity and loss
helps me to live with love.

After the color of love has been splashed on
every pore, no color leaves any impressions.
All is stunted before the giantess of love.

All are here
The moon & the stars
Still they do not light up my path!

Love came and soared me so high
The fall will only take my life.

When you are with me, let the silences rest
They have been awake all the lonely nights.

I pledged my life to love
Alas; the pangs of fate caught me young!

The roses have withered, petal by petal
Now, the thorns reign young and mighty.

Why do you shy from the pain?
It's only a prelude to birth.

Only you see that which is invisible to the self.
I am blinded by the veils of the ego.

I'll climb all ladders that lead to your heart
And the let go off them, forever!

Epilogue

Dr Pallavi Kwatra is a anesthesiologist by profession, a writer at heart. Though words are ill -equipped to accurately portray the heart's lovely landscapes, she makes some tiny humble efforts to make poetry or write her deep impressions on life and its splendorous beauties. She is deeply interested in reading about various religions, faiths and philosophies. In all her readings, she is only in awe of the similar sacredness that she encounters. She is also a Buddhist practitioner, a Reiki channel, practices kriya and hatha yoga and is proficient in other healing modalities. She holds avid interest in learning various alternative healing modalities of the mind, body and soul other than her own allopathic medicine practice. These urges were inspired in her by a life threatening medical encounter in 2010 that set her to seek deeper.Natural beauties of oceans and mountains inspire in her creativity and entice her to discover newer unchartered lands of her soul self. She strongly believes in the power of the pen to strike the heart's deepest chords to compose newer and more melodious music. Her first published book is 9 MONTHS : FROM INVOLUTION TO EVOLUTION which is a compilation of whats app conversations between 12 medical friends on various spiritual matters. It is avalaible on all leading web portals like amazon, flipkart etc. In her thinking, a writer's ode to life is his biggest asset and also his responsibility to his beloved fellowmen. In all humility, she only carries on what divine guidance has directed her to.

She can be reached out on her e mail id:
pallavi_kwatra@yahoo.com

Pallavi's beautiful book and poetry call to the heart of the Beloved whom touches every moment of life and yearns to be known through us as Grace's Radiant Love. Love reaches every space of our being and transforms its Presence into the very alchemy of Union between the Beloved and the lover. Just breath and inhale feel this intimacy of Source manifesting in your very being, breath out and exhale to be one with all of Eternity. This book invites you into the intimacy, nearness and divinity of poetic realization of your true self as Love. Pallavi's journey invites us to explore how this unfolds for her and for all of us ultimately in unique ways.

Ruahh Adya

Author Moments of Surrender

Throughout all of human existence, great wordsmiths have grappled to put language around the ineffable experience of love. In the grand tradition of the world's greatest poets, such as Rumi, Rilke, Hafiz, and others, poetess Pallavi Kwatra gives us a glimpse into the transcendent heights, and lows, that laying ourselves on love's altar delivers. Again and again, she makes herself a devotee, allowing love itself to be her guru, her master, her teacher, and her muse. From love's crescendos to love's depths of despair, she lays her heart open, making of it a portal that we can walk through to discover love's glory. Very few writers are able to so eloquently deliver the sublime delicacies that love has to offer. This is a feast to be savored poem by poem, line by line, word by word, as one would savor the rarest of delicacies. Take each poem in...let it open you, arouse you, awaken you, and deliver you to your own salvation and redemption."

Tina M. Benson,

M.A., author of international bestseller, "A Woman Unto Herself: A Different Kind of Love Story."

Notes